THE BOOK OF KELLS

The Poiema Poetry Series

Poems are windows into worlds; windows into beauty, goodness, and truth; windows into understandings that won't twist themselves into tidy dogmatic statements; windows into experiences. We can do more than merely peer into such windows; with a little effort we can fling open the casements, and leap over the sills into the heart of these worlds. We are also led into familiar places of hurt, confusion, and disappointment, but we arrive in the poet's company. Poetry is a partnership between poet and reader, seeking together to gain something of value—to get at something important.

Ephesians 2:10 says, "We are God's workmanship . . ." *poiema* in Greek—the thing that has been made, the masterpiece, the poem. The Poiema Poetry Series presents the work of gifted poets who take Christian faith seriously, and demonstrate in whose image we have been made through their creativity and craftsmanship.

These poets are recent participants in the ancient tradition of David, Asaph, Isaiah, and John the Revelator. The thread can be followed through the centuries—through the diverse poetic visions of Dante, Bernard of Clairvaux, Donne, Herbert, Milton, Hopkins, Eliot, R. S. Thomas, and Denise Levertov—down to the poet whose work is in your hand. With the selection of this volume you are entering this enduring tradition, and as a reader contributing to it.

—D. S. Martin
Series Editor

The Book of Kells

BARBARA CROOKER

Barbara Crooker

3.30.19

For Clare,
at AWP
we meet at last!
In praise of women
poets everywhere!
Slainte!
Barbara

 CASCADE *Books* · Eugene, Oregon

THE BOOK OF KELLS

The Poiema Poetry Series

Cascade Books
An Imprint of Wipf and Stock Publishers
199 W. 8th Ave., Suite 3
Eugene, OR 97401

www.wipfandstock.com

PAPERBACK ISBN: 978-1-5326-0636-6
HARDCOVER ISBN: 978-1-5326-0638-0
EBOOK ISBN: 978-1-5326-0637-3

Cataloging-in-Publication data:

Names: Crooker, Barbara, author.

Title: The Book of Kells / Barbara Crooker.

Description: Eugene, OR: Cascade Books, 2019. | The Poiema Poetry Series.

Identifiers: ISBN 978-1-5326-0636-6 (paperback). | ISBN 978-1-5326-0638-0 (hardcover). | ISBN 978-1-5326-0637-3 (ebook).

Subjects: LCSH: Poetry. | American poetry—21st century.

Classification: PS3553.R548 B62 2019 (print). |PS3553 (ebook).

Manufactured in the USA.

for Richard, who made this possible

Table of Contents

Introduction

The Book of Kells is an illuminated manuscript Gospel book in Latin, containing the four Gospels of the New Testament together with various prefatory texts and tables. It was created in a Columban monastery in either Britain or Ireland. It is believed to have been created c. 800 AD. It is a masterwork of Western calligraphy and represents the pinnacle of Insular illumination. It is also widely regarded as Ireland's finest national treasure.

The illustrations and ornamentation of the Book of Kells surpass that of other Insular Gospel books in extravagance and complexity. The decoration combines traditional Christian iconography with the ornate swirling motifs typical of Insular art. Figures of humans, animals, and mythical beasts, together with Celtic knots and interlacing patterns in vibrant colors, enliven the manuscript's pages. Many of these minor decorative elements are imbued with Christian symbolism and so further emphasize the themes of the major illustrations. The plates are numbered with an "r" or a "v" to indicate "recto" (right) or "verso" (left).

Barbara Crooker received a writing fellowship at the Tyrone Guthrie Centre, Co. Monaghan, Ireland, where she meditated on pages of the Book of Kells both in the Long Library, Trinity College, Dublin, and online.

prologue

Samhain

Night opens its woven basket, spills
spools of thread on the worn rug
of the sky. Places a silver thimble
to light the way. The old woman says,
sweep the hearth, light the fire;
winter is coming.
Look in the mirror swirled
with smoke, turn over a card,
sprinkle salt in the doorway.
A single candle flickers,
drowns in its own wax.

Newgrange

Brú na Bóinne (Valley of the Boyne, Ireland)

It's deep time here, this barrow grave five thousand years old,
where we follow like sheep behind the guide to the heart
of its cruciform center. I've never been in a space so dark.
What was it like to fear that the sun would not return,
that crops would whither, deer flee, that night's dark cloak
was all there was? But miraculously, on the lip of the solstice,
the light returned, liquid and golden, ran down the narrow corridor,
hit the back wall, splashed in the stone basin, and they knew summer
would come back, run to fruit. Light, dark, freeze, thaw, seedtime,
harvest, wheel of the year, the spiral dance. What would they make
of our device-laden lives, fossil-fueled cars, over-stocked larders?
Who stands in the dark and listens now, gaping at the stars?

one

Trinity College, the Book of Kells

10/19/13 page of the day: Portrait of St. John, folio 291v and 292r

In a dim room, the Gospel of John rises, pure gold
in the gloom: *In the beginning was the word,*
and the word was made flesh. John's seated
on a throne of ultramarine, haloed
in plaits of light. He's my tribe, a scribe,
notebook in one hand, pen in the other. Around him,
tattooed in vellum, interlace knots, no beginning
or end. The more I stare in this darkness,
the less I see, patterns too small for my retinae,
these aging eyes. Made from pigments of verdigris,
orpiment, lampblack and woad, is it a vision,
or merely a dream? Metalwork or woven ribbons,
this is the universe recast as pattern, and I draw in
a breath, Word of God on my tongue.

The Book of Kells: Chi Rho

The work, not of men, but of angels. Gerald of Wales

With quills and ink of iron gall on folded vellum,
monks in their cells labored in hives of stone,
producing pages that glistened like honey,
sweetening the word of God. On this page, the chi
commands the eye, its arm swooping to the left
in an elegant scrawl, the smaller rho and iota
nestled to the right. Knotwork fills each letter
to the brim. Three angels fly from the crossed
arms, heaven and earth intertwined, coiled spirals
connected by curves. Despite the gleam, no gold
is used, just layers of color built up like enamel.
In the interstices, creatures of air: birds and moths;
creatures of sea: fish and otters; creatures of land:
cats and mice. For the whole world was holy,
not just parts of it. The world was the Book of God.
The alphabet shimmered and buzzed with beauty.

Schilig Mhichil: a Glosa

It is hard to believe that for quite a long time—almost a hundred years—western Christianity survived by clinging to places like Skellig Michael, a pinnacle of rock eighteen miles from the Irish coast, rising seven hundred feet out of the sea.
            —Kenneth Clark

Every day, hands are creating the world,
fire is married to steel,
and canvas, linen and cotton come back
from the skirmishings of the laundries
            Pablo Neruda (translated by Alistair Reid), "In Praise of Ironing,"

They sat on hard benches in stone beehives
perched above the immaculate sea
on the steepest, most wind-battered peak,
climbing six hundred steps to the scriptoria
on rocks piled by the hand of God.
Skellig Michael, above the waters' skirl.
The Vikings somehow found them,
looted and plundered, but the monks
built again, and the word unfurled.
Every day hands are creating the world.

On this impossible crag,
this tower of slate, stark fissures,
castellated outcrops terrifying
above the brooding sea, the steps rise
between fangs of rock, a space
to chasten or elevate souls. Feel
how it was to live in a clochán,
nothing but obdurate rock above and below.
In Europe, books burned, but here were concealed.
Fire is married to steel.

8

No one could labor like this who didn't love books,
the gospel page shining, white as cotton
fresh from the laundry, a pledge that darkness
could turn into light. Even the shapes
of the letters were magical, the humps
and curves of half-uncial, insular majescule, black
ink made from soot inscribed on sheepskin,
the fabric of God's words, newly woven,
hands fast as shuttles, each simple act,
canvas, linen, and cotton come back.

Imagine a world without reading or learning;
imagine a life without books. A land ruled
by ax and sword, stones stained with blood.
No bleach or bluing to set things right; no iron
mangle to wring things clean. Cities tumbled
to rubble, books burned for warmth. Armies
looting the countryside. Only the Irish, on an island
in the icy sea, water-swirled and rock-haunted,
the ragged edge of the West, saved whole libraries
from the skirmishing of the foundries.

Book of Kells

October 19, 2013: folio 253v-254r

The text of the day is open to Luke, chapter sixteen,
verse ten. The initial N, made up of blond men

facing off, grappling and tugging at each other's beards,
becomes the first word in the section that warns us

that no servant can serve two masters. Irony intended.
Later, in beautiful insular majuscule, the open letters filled

in red and blue, we read *You cannot serve both God and money.*
I wish that these words would rise off the page, a swarm of bees,

become honey to spread on our daily bread. When the scribes
made an error, in a world before white-out, the correct word

was inserted in a box of red dots. Aren't there words today
we'd like to amend like that? In this dimly lit room, circling

glass cases, I return to view the same vellum over again,
twelve hundred years later, clear as the day it was written.

I think of Henri Nouwen: *The word is born in silence,*
and silence is the deepest response to the word.

Books

In folio 32v, Jesus sits, not on the Throne of Heaven,
but on an ordinary blue kitchen chair. He's barefoot
and holding a book. *In principio erat verbum*;
in the beginning was the Word. His hair, blond
plaits ending in Celtic twists. He's framed,
not by angels, but by farmhouse peacocks.
You can almost hear their unworldly squawks.
On other pages, we see books brandished by angels
instead of flaming swords. Or clutched to the chests
of young boys. St. Matthew is holding his gospel
like a treasure, all silver and gold, delicate tracings
on the bindings. Imagine a world where books
were scarce. Where copying was done by human hand.
Where the word itself was sacred.

In our time, it's a rush of too much: pixelated images,
the blather of television, the constant stream of the internet.
With such a torrent, nothing is important; all of it blends
and whirls. While outside my window, a blackbird
sings, its clear six notes the only sound.
They pierce me like nails. He might be saying
Listen, listen, listen. He might have flown down
to remind me that, more than anything,
my job is to pay attention.

Angels

One set of scholars believes the Book of Kells was created to honor the 200th anniversary of the death of Colum Cille (St. Columba).

In the Book of Kells, messengers are both seen and unseen:
framing the Virgin at the Nativity in all four corners;
the infant Christ, dressed as a small man, fully clothed,
on his mother's knee. The angel in the upper left
seems to be saying *Oh, my God. What have you done?*
Do you _really_ think this was a good idea?
The one on the upper right seems resigned. *You want*
to send him _where_? While the two on the bottom, crowded
behind Mary's chair, seem dwarfed by the occasion, relegated
to the corners. But they're always there. I like the angels
on the arm of the chi in the great Chi Rho; you have to tilt
the page to see them, unflagrant, hovering above.
And some angels are almost hidden, like the one
in folio 48r, hands outstretched in prayer, framed
in the diamond-shaped O of *Omnia*. What
would it have been like to live then, in the time
of Colum Cille, when angels might have been hovering
in the breathable air?

Interlinear

Let's praise the agile little animals
that flit here and there in the Vulgate text,
who can wedge in small spaces: the moth
in initial P, antenna flickering outside the line.
Or the monk on his horse, trotting right off the page.
Look, there's an otter, his mouth full of fish, and here,
a blue cat sits watchfully by. A gorgeous green lizard
slithers in the text, 72r, while a wolf pads his way
through 76v. It's a whole barnyard: chickens and mice,
hounds and hares, snakes, eagles, and stags. Animals
as decoration. Animals as punctuation. Things seen
and unseen. So let us praise all of God's creatures,
including the small and the inconsequential, all of us,
interlinear, part of the larger design.

Snake

Symbol of the resurrection, slithering and hissing
down the page. The monks believed a snake
was restored to youth whenever it shed its skin.
But then there was the snake in Genesis, the loss
of innocence, the great fall: a double-edged
sword, a forked tongue. In the Book of Kells,
some snakes are made out of abstract interlace,
while others form complete borders:
serpentine coiling interweaving fretwork tracery:
S.

The Cock and Two Hens

Ordinary barnyard chickens, a rooster and his hens, feathers
of lapis blue, copper green, scratch the ground in folio 67r, above
the parable of the sower and the seed. Did they come clucking
and pecking when they heard the grain rain down? Or did they flop
with a squawk to listen to the story? Was it corn that was thrown?
Were these the seeds that fell by the wayside? Did they fall
on deaf ears? Were there thorns ready to choke new growth,
or was it rocky ground where some sprouted among stones
but couldn't withstand the sun's hot breath? We are told
to throw our kernels on good earth and they will grow
thirty, sixty, a hundred-fold.

The chickens are not impressed with this tale. They're
interested only in filling their bellies. Like them,
we may hear, but not understand. We may see,
but not perceive. The chickens shrug, strut, continue
to hunt and peck in the gravel and dust.

Peacocks

They're everywhere in the Book of Kells,
eating grapes with lions, perched on the heads
of snakes, contorted in roundels, crammed
inside letters: languidly draped on an H
or painfully squashed in a U. The pale host
appears on their tails instead of extravagant
blue/gold/red eyes. The monks thought their flesh
incorruptible, symbol of the resurrected Christ.
Sometimes their feet are twined in grapevines
growing from chalices. Sometimes, the cup's
upside down, and flowing vines spill over.
Sometimes, you're startled into beauty:
the flare of blue fire when they open their fans.

Once, driving back north from Florida,
the world returned to black and white,
we were forced off the interstate by an accident.
A foot of snow on the ground, and more still falling.
Suddenly, as if conjured, a peacock flew
across the road in front of us, its exclamation
of blue-green iridescence all the more startling
in this colorless world. *Did we really just see that?*
we asked each other, but then the road turned
and we were back on the highway,
safely delivered, on our way home.

Cat in Folio 280R

Look at me sitting in green and gold splendor,
outlined in red dots, fitting decoration
for a royal design. I've no doubt that cats
are the finest of God's creations. I've a place
of my own on this strong piece of vellum,
four lines from the top, the best part of the page.
My garden's a heaven of strokes in a row
made by ink and the sharp tip of a feather—
birds, so delicious, I eat them for tea.
What all these humps mean, I haven't a clue;
perhaps they are mouse holes? I'll sit here
and wait. They must be important because
I'm here to guard them. Unless, of course,
something better comes by, like a butterfly
to chase or a nap in the corner. Excuse me,
I'm yawning, and there, by the fire,
is a very soft cushion, so tempting,
good night.

The Alphabet

So many open letters filled in with designs;
did the monks, like us, doodle all day?
Inside an H, there's a man whose lips help form
Jesus spoke. Two poor peacocks are pressed face-to-face
for eternity, twined inside the letter U, while two hungry lions
become R and D, yoga for felines, ever-flexible. Imagine a P
made of cat, bird, and snake. Or a snake slithered into a knot,
hissing his name. For the monks, the very shapes of the letters
were magical, this graceful insular majuscule. Inscribed
with the simplest of materials, ink into hide, each initial
coils and curls, retraces the world in vegetal wonder.

Capitals

In the Book of Kells, 2000 capitals, no two alike.
Animals, humans, plants twisted and interlaced
to form letters: petals, stems, branching patterns.
The line "Remember Lot's wife" begins
with a salty white face looking backwards, framed
in the heart of the capital. "Paying taxes to Caesar"
starts with a capital T in Latin, made of a little man
with his neck torqued and straining, his arms
outstretched, reaching through a tangle of ribbon
to catch a bird in flight. The Pharisees tried
to snare Jesus in their net, but he flew away.
The Sermon on the Mount has eight capital Bs
for *Blessed*, four of them human, four of them
swans, whose long necks outline the right-hand
side of the letter. I would like *my* letter B to be
embellished, emblazoned in orpiment, lapis lazuli,
red lead, copper green, woven out of flowers and leaves,
knots and curlicues. I would like to be scratched
into vellum with the quill of a swan, delineated
in brown oak gall. Bend me, Lord, like a human pretzel,
fit me into the form you desire. Let me shine
like crushed foil, let me become a perfect design.

Punctuation

Some parts of the Book of Kells are punctuated,
not by ordinary marks like ampersands, colons,
exclamations, commas, but like this:
a horseman's foot points like an arrow on a one-way
street, drawing the eye to the text *Et tertia die resurget.*
Instead of brackets, tiny animals. When a word didn't fit
on the line, they placed the extra syllable in the space
over the line or tucked carefully under the unfinished
word, guarded by the outstretched wing of a bird
or the front paws of a dog. The scribes called this
"putting the head under the wing" or "taking the turn
down the path."

I'd like to insert little animals into modern English:
ladybugs instead of periods, question mark earthworms,
starfish asterisks, squirrel-tail commas, and ellipses,
a fine line of industrious ants, ever marching. . . .

The Book of Kells

Here, there's no circle, only the spiral, endlessly
turning back on itself. No straight lines, only curves,
coiling, looping. There's no direct path to the Kingdom
of Heaven; it's circuitous, echoing the barrow graves
of Newgrange, indecipherable swirls, zigzags, lozenges.
Knots without end, alpha and omega, merged. Lines
that refuse to conform to a pattern, dance to their own rhythm,
lost in a maze. Here, the power's derived from the wander,
and each turn changes the rules. Turn-in-the-Path. Head-Under-Wing.
Is it possible to capture God in a furrow, snare Him within curvilinear
    lines?
Metalwork without pattern, interlace gone wild. Yet, no matter
how many twistings and turnings, it returns to the center, the still
    heart's core.

Four Men Pulling Beards

folio 188r

Two men face each other,
left arm under right leg over
right arm, each pulling the beard
of his counterpart. And this is
repeated by his friend:
under, over, yank. Beneath
them, two more men, the exact
same knot of arms and legs. Oh, what
tangled webs we weave. Is this
friendship, or an age-old quarrel?
One thing is certain: no one
wants to be the first
to let go.

Ink

It's made from what remains:
powder of oak galls, tincture
of iron, thin wine or vinegar—
a mixture mysterious as a hag's charm
or potion aflame in a cauldron.
How could these monks know in the future,
twelve hundred years later, that their hooks
and angles carved in the skin of a small herd
of calves using pens cut with feathers
would make us stop in our tracks, full of wonder,
stunned by the mystery of the alphabet,
the fastness of the Word.

Gold

Not precious metal,
but the sun: yolk
candled and cradled
inside the thin shell.
Or else it was orpiment,
called yellow arsenic,
shining loudly on the page.
Not gilt flake or leaf,
merely plain pigment,
layer upon layer.
Breath of the Holy
Spirit made visible
darkness transfigured
into light.

Kermes Red

For the Book of Kells,
monks made Kermes red, bled
from crushed bodies
of small pregnant insects.
Not the red lead of minium,
rusty red-orange, but bluer,
truer, to scarlet, to flame.
Look how its placement
makes gold gleam,
a dream of a color
that burns to set
your yearning heart
aflame.

The Scribe

Before the scriptorium, I worked in my cell,
plain simple beehive made out of rock.
Or outside in good weather: old book on one knee,
new sheepskin on the other, copying, copying.
Under the greenwood tree, listening to the cuckoo's song.

By the end of the day, my hand grows weary,
and the sharp quill starts making wobbly lines.
But I marvel how far my inky fingers have traveled,
copying these books from across the far sea.
I don't think of words, just the shapes of the letters,
as they steadily march on the plains of the page.

My pen drips brownish gall ink, makes me think
of the nut-brown ale that is waiting, along
with an apple, and a small wedge of cheese.
When darkness surrounds me, I'll take to my bed,
ready to rise with gladness tomorrow,
and, once again, take up my pen.

Complaints from Medieval Scribes

a found poem

Imagine sitting for hours at a slant desk,
copying on rough parchment with a sharpened
quill, day after lonely day. Of course you'd be
tempted to write in the margins: "That's a hard page
and a weary work to read it." "New parchment,
bad ink; I say nothing more." "The ink is thin."
"I am very cold." "Saint Patrick of Armagh,
deliver me from writing." "Thank God
it will soon be dark." "Oh, my hand." "Now
that I've written the whole thing: for Christ's
sake give me a drink."

two

Ireland

A brown hare washes her face
in the lane while the hare in the moon
looks on. The hare in the moon
carries an egg, new cycle of life
that comes in the spring. But now
it's autumn, the sky closing in,
fir trees inking footprints
on the gray silk sky. A luminous sky,
tattered with crows. Two swans,
ruffled lilies, float in the lake's bright bowl.
Some fairy's touched all the trees overnight,
turned them orange, yellow, and red. All of
the green fields are clotted with sheep. What
is this world, but the body of God?

Journey

at the Tyrone Guthrie Centre, Annaghmakerrig, Ireland

Blackbirds chuff the dull sky,
color of roof slates on this grey day.
Yesterday, sheets of rain lashed
the bus going north. In the terminal,
lashings of tea. After the rain stopped,
out for a walk; autumn, and chestnut
and oak leaves litter the ground brown
and gold. The quiet, broken only by
swans, whose startled wing beats,
low notes of a cello, stir the air.
Above the lake, firs murmur
their resinous dreams.

Tyrone Guthrie Centre

Annaghmakerrig, Ireland

And so, as the rain comes down in great sheets,
I'm having tea in the drawing room of a manor
house turned into a retreat, pretending
I actually live here, with a carved marble
fireplace, gold-crusted mirror, fruitwood
bookcase, parquet floors. There's an old
wooden radio off in the corner, and I turn the dial,
think I hear Glenn Miller, Artie Shaw. The window's
a screen of pointillist drops that jitter and jive their way
down the glass. It's October, and the rose hips are swollen,
artillery shells about to explode. Someone's lived by this lake
going back to prehistory. The wind whistles, a fife, as it blows
round the stones. My mug of tea is growing cold.

Lake Annaghmakerrig

Guzzling the current, against it all muscle and slur
In the finland of perch, the fenland of alder, on air

That is water, on carpets of Bann stream, on hold
In the everything flows and steady go of the world.
                    Seamus Heaney, "Perch"

After rain, the lake spreads out its grey water,
bolts of silk rippling in the feather-tipped breeze.
There's a chatter of rooks in the chestnuts, their
coal-black bodies, dark stars sucking light
from all that surrounds them: serrated
chestnut leaves copper and amber,
the grass below, a glint of green plush.
The rain's thin music has set the world humming,
small stanzas of fishes, slim as a whisper, are
guzzling the current, against it, all muscle and slur.

The rain returns, pocking the surface,
dimpling the skin of the fishes' grey sky.
Does its rattle and chatter bother their dreaming,
their little thoughts, as they fin on their way?
Or is it just static, an untuned radio, television
before cable, turning rabbit ears here and there,
trying to conjure an image from snow? Hiss and trickle,
the drops hit my window, then slowly meander their way
down the pane. Everything's liquid, a watery prayer:
in the finland of perch, the fenland of alder, on air.

Then the wind picks up, whistling round corners,
flinging the rain in tight parallel lines. The glass
of the windows become a grey blur. But stretched out
before me, the grass is pure emerald,
thirstily drinking what comes from the sky: rain

34

that falls on the just and unjust, the young and the old.
Out in the larger world, bicker of politics—the rich
keep on scheming, dreaming up ways to corner the market,
for a future whose currency will be in rivers. The gold
that is water, on carpets of Bann stream, on hold.

Now today, the sun has turned up its high beams, casting
deep shadows on the gleaming lawn. The rooks are giddy,
drunk on the sunshine, gossiping noisily from tree
to tree; across the pale lake, tips of the rowans
are starting to flame. The Celts who once lived here believed
that the body's an echo of soul. Today, clouds swirled
like cream in blue coffee; it's hard to imagine our soon-to-be
breakdowns, the greed of the powerful, the black birds
of drought. Instead, there's the fish, rippled, empearled
in the everything flows and steady go of the world.

Small Song for October

Look, the lake blooms with late roses.
Look again, you'll see they're the bodies of swans.
The trees continue their slow change of color,
red, gold and orange; soon they'll be gone.
The lawn's on green fire, can't be any greener.
Soon, there'll be a chill in the air. Meanwhile,
the swans unpetal their plumage, paddling
their way up and down the long lake. And we,
who are neither migratory nor native, feel a lift
as they loft themselves into the sky.

Swans

But now they drift on the still water,
Mysterious, beautiful;
Among what rushes will they build,
By what lake's edge or pool
                    William Butler Yeats, "The Wild Swans at Coole"

Sun mixed with clouds, and the wind kicks up,
ruffling the calm of the tree-ringed lake,
whose surface shatters, fractures
in shards of glittering shadow and light.
I was dull as the slate-bottomed
clouds, sunk in torpor,
so I pulled on my boots, went for a walk
down the rhododendrons' graveled path,
where I startled to see swans, buoyant white flowers;
now they drift on the still water.

They float on the surface, self-contained
lilies, their plumage buoyant
clouds drifting by.
Who can forget the sound of their voices:
discordant brass trumpets, golden
as the chestnut trees ringing the banks? Full
moon that evening, swan of ebony waters, both
of them, gliding soundlessly by.
Both of them gorgeous, gardenias in a bowl:
Mysterious, beautiful.

It's a mystery, isn't it, these birds that mate
for life? While we don't seem to know how to stick it,
marriages ending, families that fracture, children
distant and estranged. Look at these swans,
who court beak to beak, thick necks nearly forming a heart.
Their cygnets stay with them all winter through the chill,

37

eating water plants, gleaning in pastures, taking
whatever comes their way. Honking and flapping, warning
off predators. *Beware our snapping beaks*, they blare and trill.
Among what rushes will they build?

Three years ago, we went to the Burren,
walking around the limestone karst. Almost lunar,
those slabs of gray stone, crisscrossed with cracks
where alpine flowers bloom. Then we saw, on a map,
Lady Gregory's park, and we drove to the turlough
hoping to see the wild swans at Coole.
The trees were in their autumn beauty, and the water
did mirror the sky. And you and I felt something subtle
moving inside us, something coming close to renewal,
by that lake's edge or pool.

Whooper Swans

In Monaghan
they say
there are no
horizons.

The glaciers
left drumlins
long rolling hills.
In the green fields,

cows amble,
a black-and-white
river, and on the long lake,
a whiting of swans

as if
two clouds
drifted down
from the heavens,

citron beaks
charcoal feet
meringue wings
a snowdrift in flight

as if
full-blown peonies
in ruffled petals
decided to settle,

burst into
bloom on the lake.
And where are we
standing, here in this

                    picture?
              Flat-footed,
              astonished,
         and about to take wing.

Annaghmakerrig

The Tyrone Guthrie Centre

Up on the second floor, in a manor house
converted to studio use, my four tall windows
converse with the sky. In the middle distance,
the lake spreads her skirts; an etching of fir trees
stretches behind. Right now, the wind whistles
down corners; inside, it's warm, safe from the rain.
Rain, that keeps sending out messages, rat-a-tat-tat
as it knocks on the panes. Soon, I'll climb into bed
and lie sheeted: firm mattress, thick pillows,
comforter stuffed with the feathers of geese.
Wild geese, whose wings will fly me
over night's endless river,
back to my love across the far sea.

three

Small Prayer

Ireland, late October, and first frost settles on the lawn.
Yesterday, the gardener on his tractor mowed
in concentric circles, a Celtic knot at the center
of his design. Now in the grooves, ice crystals
set off the pattern, illuminate it as surely
as monks in their cells. Up from the lake,
a fairy mist rises, and whooper swans bugle up
the dawn, which flushes the clouds pink and gold.
On this new day, may I walk out singing, open
to what's never happened before. Let me be grateful.
Let me pay attention. And then when evening
closes the shutters, may I sail through the night
on the back of a swan.

Magpies

Magpie on the lawn, and I am transfixed
by its exotic look: stark black and white
feathers, jutting tail, its strut like a peacock
on the glittering grass that spills a handful
of emeralds before him. *One is for sorrow*,
the old nursery rhyme goes, and I look for a partner,
hoping for joy. Oily feathers glossed purple
and green, snowy shoulders, chest, and wingtips,
motley and pied. He doesn't need the rest
of the spectrum, the gaudy rainbow's pennants and flags.
He knows the world is black and white. See him swoop,
searching for treasure: bottlecaps, gum wrappers, pennies,
the glitter the rest of the world discards. This gray day
brightens because of his antics, and look, here
comes *joy* winging to join him, just when
I thought it was no longer possible. . . .

Fuchsia

Here in county Monaghan, they ring,
fuchsia's bells, burning in their branches,
lanterns in the dark. *Tears of God*, they're called
by the Irish, but if He's crying, then sorrow is scarlet
and purple, making me think of elegance, not dolor
and dirge. At home, frost will have scorched
these bright colors, but here, they blaze in perpetual
light. Tropical plants in a country of stone,
nurtured by the warm current of the North Atlantic.
A bush made of miracles, endlessly burning.

Almost

--for Clare

In this house, in which you are absent,
I wish I could say what it's like to be here,
drinking tea in a blue-patterned mug
while rain mutters and spatters
the flagstones. All day long, the wind
has been howling, tries to sneak
through a crevice or crack.
What's it like where you are now,
far beyond the land of the living?
Our world is so much less with your absence,
like the smudge the moon makes
as it brushes the sky. It feels as if you're
nearby, just out of sight, a floater, a speck,
at the far edge of consciousness. The veil's
pulled thin here in Ireland, a translucence
that might be crossed if only I knew
the right words, the patterns, how to read
the leaves, how to climb the ladder of stars.

Reel

Maybe night is about to come
calling, but right now
the sun is still high in the sky.
It's half-past October, the woods
are on fire, blue skies stretch
all the way to heaven. Of course,
we know winter is coming, its thin
winding sheets and its hard narrow bed.
But right now, the season's fermented
to fullness, so slip into something
light, like your skeleton; while these old
bones are still working, my darling,
let's dance.

Laundry

. . .the fabric like a sail was cross-wind,
they made a dried-out undulating thwack.
So we'd stretch and fold and end up hand to hand
for a split second as if nothing happened.
                  Seamus Heaney, "Clearances," No. 5

A wild windy day, we hung sheets on the line,
pegged them down with clothespins, let them flap
free, enormous white birds. We'd been at odds,
all sixes and sevens, not taking time to talk
or touch. So easy to go to our separate spaces,
you, in the recliner watching TV, me with a thin
book, listening to jazz. But out on the rope, our
laundry entwined, your socks running off with my
silk negligee, black bras and tee shirts, all of our linen:
the fabric like a sail in a cross-wind.

And so, in the wind, our laundry commingled,
and little by little, we came back again. It's
hard to recall how it was when it started,
our bodies so eager to burst into flame. But now
it's dead embers, dry kindling, cold ash.
I'm remembering before we met, back
to living alone with a small child, not enough
money or food on the table, wearing two sweaters, lowering
the heat. I just heard the sheets, sun-warm from the rack;
they made a dried-out undulating thwack.

So after all those days at cross-purposes, here
we are, hauling in garments that smell
of wind, cut grass, the sun's hot breath.
Together, we sort: his/hers/ours, what
goes in the cupboard at the top of the stairs.
Something impromptu, something not planned,

but we found a rhythm that almost seemed
natural, returning shirts to their drawers, hanging
up pants. Then the bed loomed, a plain from a faraway land,
where we could stretch and fold, end up hand to hand.

On either side of the divide, we stretched out
the bottom sheet, tucked in the corners, smoothed
the wrinkles. Then the top sheet floated up
when we shook it, as if still filled
with the breath of the wind. And last, the quilt,
bought when we weren't using love as a weapon.
I gave it a tug, pulling you closer; your hand touched
mine, a way out of the maze we were trapped in—
for a split second as if nothing happened.

Late October, Ireland

A sad air's best for night as you mope about
the house, closing windows, checking doors.
Slow, cumulative strokes of the violin bow,
the most ruminative notes that can be coaxed.
        Dennis O'Driscoll, "Nocturne Op. 2"

The late afternoon light's the color of tea,
and I sink in an armchair, open a book.
Outside my window, the leaves are on fire,
color of embers when flames have died down.
Night comes too early, curtains are drawn.
Lamps cast bright circles, the sun's bulb's burnt out,
and the darkness seems total, shadows that you
could spread with a knife. Turn on the radio, listen
to opera. October should be played on a violin, no doubt.
A sad air's best for night as you mope about.

A night sleepless and seemingly endless,
dark dreams no rational thought can dispel.
This is the end of the Celtic year's cycle, and the veil
between living and dead grows filmy and thin. Every year
one or two friends have gone missing, those who
have rowed on the outgoing tide. Shadows pool on the floor,
while outside, it's thick as a black tom cat's fur.
There's nothing to do, as I toss on my pillow, so I walk
down the hall, make my rounds, shutting drawers—secure
the house, closing windows, checking doors.

Morning comes crashing, put on the kettle. Pour me another,
it's been a bad night. In the garden, there are apples
ready for cider, or perhaps something harder
to ward off the dark. Make no mistake, now,
summer is over, days are far shorter, the wind
has a chill. Leaves on the aspen have all turned to yellow,

the color of money, coin in the potato. There's a coal
in the turnip to light our way forward. We put on masks
so the dead will not see. Place a lock of your hair in the fire, so.
Slow cumulative strokes of the violin bow.

The wind's violin howls a tune down the chimney.
Let's play Snap Apple and eat curly kale. Extinguish
the flame on your hearth, light another. Welcome
the new year, there's milk in the pail. Strike a match,
light the oven, and mix up some Barnbrack. Somebody
lucky will find the gold ring. Open the whiskey and give us a toast:
to dear friends departed, let's call out their names.
Rosin the fiddle and play us a tune. Twisted steel strings,
body of maple, music the finest that Ireland can boast,
the most ruminative notes that can be coaxed.

Retreat

~*Tyrone Guthrie Centre, Annaghmakerrig, Ireland*

Hooray for this day, clouds racing by
deckled with gold leaf, and pines that have
inked themselves onto the sky. Let's thank
the tea leaves for yielding their tannins,
released by the kettle's steam. And the leaves
on the trees, three cheers, for changing into colors
crayoned by a child: Burnt Siena. Raw Umber.
Goldenrod. Red Orange. I'm grateful to the gas
burner that bloomed with blue petals cooking
my porridge, to the cows in green pastures
for making the cream. Later, I know I'll be grateful
for lunch, red and green lettuce blessed with oil,
slivers of tomatoes, ham on the side. And one yellow
pear, a treasury of gold, its sweetness married to the salt
tang of Cashel Blue. Applause for the walk that I took
in the woodlands, ancient trees rising from fern-covered
ground. And the long lake, its waters a mirror, reflecting
two swans. Hats off! for the kingfisher I just caught a glimpse
of, exclamation of turquoise, bluer than blue. Let's not forget
about dinner, a sea bass so tender it fell off the plate, surrounded
by root vegetables, stars of the season: carrots, turnips, potatoes
crusted with cheese. But wait, there's an encore, a platter of rhubarb,
a blanket of meringue. Most of all, there's the pleasures
of the table: good conversation, the music of forks and spoons
hitting the plates. And at the end of the day, there we are,
sprinkled with starlight and a darkness that covers us, tucks us
in tight. Tomorrow, there's another day coming, not quite like
this one, but look, clouds are blushing, and here comes the sun.

Reading the Leaves

The future will come, I tell myself,
and it won't be pretty, with its aches
and sags, the body's sure decline.
So I hold on to this radiant
morning, the sun as it turns the dial
of the lake up to "glitter," polishes the grass
til it shines like a traffic light signaling go.
Blackbirds flash in and out of the oaks,
saw the air into ribbons that weave
with each gust of the wind. Even the tea
in my cup shines pure amber. And then,
there's the miraculous mixture of digital data,
electrons and photons, that later this evening
will connect me to you.

Artist Retreat, Ireland

Last night, we stayed up until two, drinking wine, telling stories, laughing. Someone played folk music on the guitar. I wanted to stay here, keep going, keep writing, but a poem I was working on needed an image, so I called my husband in Pennsylvania, asked him to describe for me what was in the air between my cell phone and his. I was expecting a long line of science, a string of jargon, something involving molecules and frequencies. When he answered, *the distance,* I knew in my heart it was time to come home.

Residency

a gigan

Autumn again, and a cold wind is blowing,
stripping gold leaves from the coppery beech.

I'm here alone, there's an ocean between
us, the cold north Atlantic, the color
of grief. Outside my window, an armada

of clouds, gunmetal gray, obscuring the sky.
Here, there's no news, only the weather, so I'm

getting my gossip from the whispers of aspens
that glitter like coins at the top of the lane. Here,

rowans are sacred, fairy rings bring protection.
Autumn again, let the cold wind blow

off the clouds, bring back cobalt skies.
I should be lonely; instead, it's a respite,
steeped in my work like a pot full of tea.

The wind keeps on saying *It's time to come home
now*; I'll be on that plane, but I won't be the same.

four

Gorse

Traveling north from Dublin, both sides of the highway
roll out in every shade of green, while along the berm
or flush against stone walls: the bright splash of daffodils.
On barren hillsides, the gorse is in bloom, furze
covering the heath, a heap of gold. After the billow
and build of storm clouds, lightning's piercing needles,
the tumult and cadence of the rain, perhaps this, then,
is rainbow's end: not glittering treasure, a hoard of coins,
but instead, thorny bushes growing where nothing else
can flourish, blooming for all they're worth,
just because they can.

Crocosmia

We saw them everywhere in the west of Ireland,
showy spikes of red-orange flowers, grass-like
leaves, gladiola's more demure cousin. But glads
are flirty debutantes, rainbow-colored, ruffles galore.
While Crocosmia are plain half-slips, sticking
to their side of the color wheel: red-orange-yellow.
What they lack in variety, they make up in reliability,
tough enough to survive Irish winters. Corms
that can weather the cold. Graceful arches,
with catalog names like: *Irish Sunset, Irish Dawn,*
Coppertips, Falling Stars. Come spring,
they'll ignite their green fire. Praise the power
of the small and hardy. The resurrection rising
out of duff and detritus. Watch their slow
small fires burn.

Beginning

Monks worked on the monastery farm until the bell
from the round tower summoned them to prayer. . . .
George Otto Simms, Exploring the Book of Kells

I'm here at this plain oak desk, black slate insert, two large
windows looking out at a green hillside brazen with daffodils:
Ireland, early spring. Three pairs of blackbirds, in the bare trees,
chuckling companionably, remind me that I am alone.
Off to the left, a rectangular tower that isn't calling me to prayer.
Unless, as the monks have said, *ora et labora*, work is a form
of prayer. But here I am, empty-handed, open-hearted,
scratching black lines on yellow paper, and hoping that somehow,
like the newly-hatched frogs in the ornamental pond,
I will be able to croak my way into song.

For Geri

in memory of Geri Rosenzweig

> *The door was open and the house was dark*
> *Wherefore I called his name, although I knew*
> *The answer this time would be silence*
> *That kept me standing listening while it grew*
>   Seamus Heaney, "The Door Was Open and the House was Dark"

I open my email, find a post from you,
except it's signed by your younger son Paul.
He said *suddenly and unexpectedly* you were gone,
and I became a flame felled by a gust
of wind. You and I exchanged every poem
written in the past forty years, every mark
we'd made on paper: the good, the bad,
the ugly, we used to joke. But now, there's no
inbox where you've gone, no note that I can start.
The door was open, and the house was dark.

My heart is heavy, and the screen is black.
I've finished something new: a bulb
that shoots a stalk, then the green fire
of leaves, tongued flame of blossom,
all the more striking against the snow.
I never send a poem out until you
take a look, make comments: "loverly,"
or "Can you lose this line?" But now there's no reply.
I *could* hit "Send," pretend that it'd go through,
wherefore I called your name, although I knew.

In the middle of a friendship, who thinks of endings?
Each poem of yours made me look forward to the next.
They journeyed back to Ireland, your family, the buttons
on your father's coat, your mother's kettle, the birds

whistling in hedgerows and lanes. Your address
remains in my contact list, plain evidence
of your existence. Denial says you're busy or away,
not checking mail. I compose a long letter, subject:
Catching Up, press "Enter," believe in this pretense.
The answer this time would be silence.

How can you be gone? And so abruptly.
Okay, you smoked. So what?
Your life was rich with family, grandkids,
poems. The manuscript unfinished.
Submissions in the mail. So many strings
untied. How you loved summer, hated it when days drew
short, the shadows longer. Once you wrote about a long-gone lily
that, like Orpheus, came back from the dead. From bare ground,
unexpected bloom. It returned; could you?
I'm left standing, listening while it grew.

Dusk

In the twilight gathering like wool, a lavender mist
knits itself behind the landscaped hill, which is green
and on fire, stitched with the bright gold buttons
of daffodils. No wonder Wordsworth was struck
dumb. I was away from home, feeling lonely
as an etc. Getting, maybe, too old for wandering.
As the light faded, the bare trees stood in relief,
became starkly more beautiful . . . .

Daily News

The ordinary world. Lights on, shades drawn
at dusk. Pea soup in a slow cooker. Frost
in the garden. Fire in the gas grate. Turn off
the television. Don't let car bombings, mass shootings,
political spewings in. This is *our* history: you, me,
the flames, the cat. The rest is static and noise.
Outside, the stars have chalked their stories
on the sky's dark slate. The street is empty,
and the house is warm.

Ogham

Ogham was a medieval alphabet for writing short messages and transcriptions, often written on wood. Each of the letters stands for a native Irish plant or tree.

Q is for apple, greeny of leaf
B is for birch tree, white in relief

L is for rowan, favored by thrushes
H is for hawthorn, planted by houses

M is for bramble, covered in thorns
D is for oak and its many acorns

G is for ivy, forever green
N is for ash, seeds of winged keys

Z is for blackthorn, its harvest of sloes
T is for holly, found in hedgerows

C is for hazel, its lambs tail catkins
S is for willow that sways in the wind

F is for fern that grows in deep woods
R is for elder, whose berries are food

I is for yew, hardwood that endures
O is for hillsides covered in furze

U is for heath, that bees mine for honey
Ng is for broom, that blooms where it's sunny

E is for aspen, that quakes in the breeze
A is for pine, with needles for leaves

Planting

Between my finger and my thumb
The squat pen rests, as snug as a gun.
Under my window a clear rasping sound
When the spade sinks into gravelly ground:
                    Seamus Heaney, "Digging"

Saint Patrick's Day, and cold. But time, where I live,
to plant peas. I scrape the grainy dregs
of snow with my hoe, try to pry some dirt
loose, still hard and full of pebbles and frost.
Each divot, a small grave, waits to receive
its hard gray nubbin, which looks dead, dumb
as a rock, and yet, given time, rain, longer days,
. some dark magic will spark a shoot,
a root, will push the earth aside. I rub a crumb
between my finger and my thumb.

Between my fingers, on this gray March day,
I roll the paper packet shut, tamp down each pock
of soil dark with compost and leaf meal.
It takes a leap of faith to believe in June, green
grass, blue skies, roses and honeysuckle
filling the air. To believe in the return of the sun,
that somehow, it will coax vines up the rusty
wire fence that tries and fails to keep out deer.
I go inside to write when gardening's done.
The squat pen rests, as snug as a gun.

But guns are on my mind, and how can they not?
Each day, another shooting on the news. My grandchildren
practice drills: *Shelter in place*, have to pretend there's
a shooter in their school. Is this not trauma, too?
More people shot by toddlers than by terrorists, and yet
Americans persist in clinging to their guns. Come around

69

to the airport, see the young men with AK45s. Do you feel
safer? I sure don't. Outside my window, a cold wind
harrows the daffodils; they scatter on the ground.
Under my window a clean rasping sound.

My skin feels rasped while listening to the news.
Another plane hijacked, another politician frothing
at the mouth. But nothing changes. Except the weather,
with storms coming in from the west; early spring
in Pennsylvania. Amidst the horror, the steady rain
of bad news, the worry over climate change, coastlines drowned
as ice caps melt, oceans rise, the only thing
I know how to do is tend my garden, turn over the dirt
in even rows, drill in the seed, pat it down,
let the spade sink into gravelly ground.

Easter Sunday, 2016

On the centenary of the Uprising, we tour
a Georgian house, Florence Court, home
of the Earls of Enniskillen, part of the Protestant
Ascendancy. We're Americans, don't understand
the significance of this date. Instead, we take it all in:
Palladian windows, baroque plasterwork, ornate
silver service, hand-painted porcelain.

Downstairs in the servants' quarters:
the wine cellar housing hundreds of bottles, the room
set aside for polishing, another room just for china.
A staff of twenty-four for this small family.
Servants were invisible, had to scuffle down cold
corridors with coal scuttles, heavy trays of food,
enter the dining room from behind an Oriental screen.
In the hall, the omnipresent bells, still waiting
to be rung.

Later, we read the *Irish Times*, see snapshots of Dublin,
parents bringing their children to the General Post Office,
where you can still feel the bullet holes. This is not the Fourth
of July: no fireworks, barbecues, marching bands,
just a nation sobered by the civil war that followed,
the streets of blood, where, Yeats wrote,
a terrible beauty is born.

We leave in a downpour, and then the sun comes out.
An unironic rainbow, translucent and fragile,
follows us on a road that had been cratered
and bombed during The Troubles, but is now
paved over, smooth macadam all the way home.

Linguistics

I hold a glass of Irish whisky in my hand
which warms the amber liquid, smooth as silk
whisked through the smoke of a peat fire.
It slides down my throat, and I feel my tongue dissolve.

*****

Yesterday, I met a man walking his dogs: a white terrier
and a red setter. I asked if I could pet them: *Oh, not the setter.*
He's wicked as a weasel, that one. At breakfast, I asked Ciaran
about the weather: *It's supposed to be fair. Except when it isn't.*
Mary-Alice wished me good morning. *What better day*
could this be? We asked about the way to Belfast:
Go on down the bendy road. Soon, you'll come to a sign.
Signs are everywhere, but I need help to translate them.

*****

Outside the window, the grass is speaking a new dialect,
the language of green, and the daffodils start to mutter,
expressing themselves in the arcane syntax of the wind.

Morning Tea

I came downstairs for Lavina's scones, butter-ready
from the oven, crusty and cratered, awaiting their dollop
of jam. The morning clouds had whipped themselves up
to a billow, mounds of soft cream. The plink plink
song of a chaffinch dotted the air like currants. Daffodils,
pats of butter on thin stems, did their little dance, and the edible
world spread its feast before me on the fresh green tablecloth.
Oh, how delicious, this sweet Irish spring.

Cootehill

for Gretchen Mccullough and Jacinta O'Reilly

The grass smoldered, green and on fire, and the daffodils
did their bob-and-weave, flickery yellow flames.
But the day grew stormy, wind howling down the chimney,
and the rain let go in great silver sheets. Inside the pub,
a peat and log fire, and the glasses of Guinness
stood tall, creamy heads, dark bodies, and a way
of taking off the chill. We had brown bread
and butter, fish stew, talk; time stretched,
relaxed, grew slack. Away from home and lonely,
a little spark began burning in the hard rocky lump
of coal I was calling my heart.

Acknowledgments

All Roads Lead, "Tyrone Guthrie Centre, Ireland," "Almost"

Anglican Theological Review, "Capitals"

Arts, "Small Prayer"

Askew, "Cootehill"

Assisi, "The Cock and Two Hens," "Snake," "The Cat in Folio 280R"

Blueline, "Dusk"

The Christian Century, "Book of Kells," "Angels," "Punctuation," "Books"

Common Ground, "Magpies," "Whooper Swans"

Crab Creek Review, "Laundry"

In Touch, "The Book of Kells: Chi Rho"

The Innisfree Poetry Journal, "Reel," "Gorse," "The Daily News"

Good Works Review, "Journey"

The MacGuffin, "Ink," "Gold," "Kermes Red"

Mezzo Cammin, "Late October, Ireland," "Residency" (published as "Writer's Retreat"), "Lake Annaghmakerrig," "For Geri," and "Ogham"

Michigan Quarterly Review, "Linguistics"

One, "Sceilig Mhichíl"

The Paterson Poetry Review, "Retreat"

Perspectives, "Complaints from Medieval Monks," "The Book of Kells"

Presence, "Trinity College, the Book of Kells"

Rose Red Review, "Samhain," "Newgrange"

Relief, "Ireland," "Peacocks"

Rock & Sling, "Easter Sunday, 2016"

Seminary Ridge Review, "Interlinear," "Four Men Pulling Beards"

Stillwater, "Crocosmia"

Summerset Review, "Reading the Leaves," "Artist Retreat, Ireland," "Small Song for October"

St. Katherine Review, "The Alphabet"

US One Worksheets, "Morning Tea"

The Valparaiso Poetry Review, "Swans"

Verse-Virtual, "Beginning"

The Christian Century nominated "Book of Kells" for the 2014 Associated Church Press Awards, where it won third prize.

Many thanks to the Tyrone Guthrie Centre, Annaghmakerrig, Ireland, for two residencies which allowed me to complete this work, and to my boon companions who enriched my time there:
Sue Healy, Maeve Ingoldsby, Deidre Kinnehan, Steve Wall, David O'Donoghue, Janet Pierce, Jacinta O'Reilly, Gretchen McCullough, Susanne Hegmann, and David Power. And to the Virginia Center for the Creative Arts for the space and time to help me finish the manuscript. Also thanks to Geri Rosenzweig, Marjorie Stelmach, Barbara Reisner, Kathleen Moser, and Dorothy Ryan for their comments on the poems in draft; to my editor at Cascade Books, D.S. Martin, for his guidance and enthusiasm, and to Mike Mirarchi, for having the sharpest eyes on the planet.

The Poiema Poetry Series